A PORTRAIT OF
NOTTINGHAM

JANET AND PETER ROWORTH

HALSGROVE

First published in Great Britain in 2006

Title page photograph: A sample of Nottingham lace.

British Library Cataloguing-in-Publication Data
A CIP record for this title is available from the British Library

ISBN 1 84114 539 4
ISBN 978 1 84114 539 6

HALSGROVE
Halsgrove House
Lower Moor Way
Tiverton, Devon EX16 6SS
Tel: 01884 243242
Fax: 01884 243325
email: sales@halsgrove.com
website: www.halsgrove.com

Printed and bound by D'Auria Industrie Grafiche Spa, Italy

ACKNOWLEDGEMENTS

We wish to thank Roly Smith, Editorial Manager for Halsgrove, for his guidance and editorial help. Also to John Ellison for generously allowing access to the Trent Bridge cricket ground when Nottinghamshire were playing Warwickshire.

Introduction

Mention Nottingham and most people think of the wicked sheriff safely tucked away in his castle while Robin Hood and his band of Merry Men roamed the surrounding forest, robbing the rich to give to the poor. So today visitors to the city flock to see the castle and be photographed at the Robin Hood statue. While the original medieval castle has long gone, the walls and gatehouse remain, topping the tall sandstone cliffs which are such a feature of the city. The walls now surround a mansion built by the Duke of Newcastle, which was turned into a municipal art gallery in the late nineteenth century.

Tucked underneath the cliff is reputedly the oldest inn in England, The Old Trip to Jerusalem, possibly named for the Crusaders who gathered there before journeying to the Holy Land. The inn and the neighbouring Brewhouse Yard Museum, like many of the older buildings in Nottingham, have caves excavated into the soft sandstone rock. In the past these were used mainly for storage but in the Second World War they made convenient air-raid shelters.

Beyond the castle is an area known as 'The Park', an exclusive residential suburb. It was created in the nineteenth century by the Duke of Newcastle, and the large architect-designed properties were favoured by the city's wealthy citizens. Many of the houses have now been converted into flats, but The Park retains its privacy with imposing entrance gates.

While the castle stands on one hill, the parish church of St Mary was founded on another. Close to the church is the unique area known as the Lace Market. This name does not adequately describe the amazing Victorian brick warehouses and offices that were built by the wealthy lace manufacturers to impress their customers, and from which they despatched lace products across the world. In the twentieth century the lace industry collapsed, but these remarkable buildings have recently been given a new lease of life as apartments, offices, bars, and part has become New College Nottingham.

In the centre of the city is the large open space of the Old Market Square, one of the stopping points for the tram system which brings visitors in from the north and from the M1. This was the original site for the famous Goose Fair, now held each October on the Forest Recreation Ground. Overlooking the square is the Council House, with its classical façade and domed roof reminiscent of St Paul's Cathedral in the capital.

Radiating from here are the streets which make up the retail heart of the city and lead to the modern shopping malls of Victoria Centre and Broad Marsh. It was in a herbalist's shop on Goose Gate in the 1870s that Jesse Boot began his working career. He later started to manufacture pharmaceutical products and by the 1930s Boots the Chemist shops could be found throughout the UK.

Like most cities, Nottingham has buildings from many periods which reflect a range of architectural styles. The timber-framed Severns House was saved from demolition and rebuilt near the castle, while the Salutation Inn also retains its medieval appearance. There are still many elegant and attractive Georgian buildings along Castle Gate and Low, Middle and High Pavement which remain from a period when this was the fashionable place for a town house.

In the Victorian period two great architects, Watson Fothergill and Thomas Chambers Hine, were responsible for some of the most grand and ornately decorated buildings. Then in the twentieth century, concrete replaced brick, and now glass is used extensively to create some stunning modern designs like the new Royal Concert Hall and the Magistrates' Court. The latter is part of the re-development of the canal waterfront which has made this an attractive area in which to live and work.

The city can boast two universities. The University of Nottingham is based at Lenton on a site donated by Sir Jesse Boot, later Lord Trent. It continues to expand and includes the teaching hospital of Queens Medical Centre. Nottingham Trent University was an amalgamation of the former technical and art colleges and it now occupies an extensive site north of the city centre.

Today, Nottingham is not just a thriving city and university town, it is an important cultural centre, with theatres, cinemas, concert halls and live entertainment venues. Its sporting facilities include the National Ice Centre, the famous Trent Bridge cricket ground, the football stadiums of Notts County and Nottingham Forest, and at Holme Pierrepont, the huge lake of the National Water Sports Centre. The city also benefits from the extensive parkland around Wollaton Hall, which itself houses a natural history and industrial museum.

We have enjoyed exploring Nottingham and we hope that our collection of photographs illustrates a modern, exciting city. But they also show a city with a long and interesting past, which is reflected in the variety of buildings which can be found on every street. We found there was much more to Nottingham than merely its associations with the legendary hero, Robin Hood.

Janet and Peter Roworth
May 2006

City of Nottingham skyline
The domed roof of the Council House, reminiscent of St Paul's Cathedral in London,
stands above the old and new buildings of the city centre.

The Council House, Old Market Square
The Council House is a modest name for a
very grand building of stunning white Portland
stone. With its classical façade and dome,
it officially opened in 1929, and houses the
council chambers, committee rooms and offices.

Floral display, Old Market Square
Nottingham is justly proud of its fine floral displays which
bring welcome colour to the city centre.

Lion statue, Old Market Square
This is one of a pair of lions which guard the front of the
Council House and look out onto the magnificent
open space of the Old Market Square.

Exchange Arcade
Situated behind the Council House the arcade is an exclusive fashion centre under an elegant glass roof.

Roof paintings, Exchange Arcade
There are four paintings under the domed roof at the centre of the Arcade, which depict scenes from Nottingham's history.

Long Row
This has always been one of the main shopping streets in the city, a site for departmental stores and fashion outlets.

Opposite: **View of King and Queen Streets**
Sandwiched between King Street on the right, and Queen Street on the left, is a Victorian building
designed by Alfred Waterhouse for the Prudential Assurance Company.

Above and opposite: **Flying Horse Walk, The Poultry**
For several hundred years this old half-timbered building was a public house and hotel,
but in 1987 it became the façade of a new shopping arcade.

Once called The Traveller's Inn, it is not known why the hotel was re-named The Flying Horse,
but a statue remains to mark the entrance to the new shopping arcade.

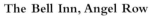

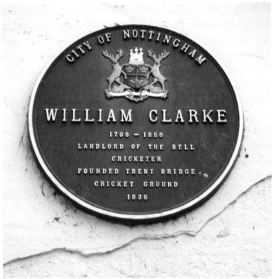

Plaque on the Bell Inn
William Clarke, who lived from 1798 to 1856, was the landlord of the Bell Inn. He was also a keen cricketer and the founder of Trent Bridge cricket ground.

The Bell Inn, Angel Row
A timber-framed building dating back to the late fifteenth century, the Bell Inn has been a public house and wine shop since the mid eighteenth century.

A tram crossing Angel Row
The modern tramway system of Nottingham Express Transit was opened in March 2004. It provides a regular
and very convenient service to visitors entering the city from the north and from the M1,
with various drop-off points including the Old Market Square and the Station.

The Malthouse public house, Victoria Street
This fine red-brick building, now known as the Malthouse public house, was once the home
of Lewis and Grundy, wholesale ironmongers.

Lewis and Grundy Clock, the Malthouse public house
The clock was a clever piece of advertising. In its working days, the two blacksmiths
marked each quarter hour by hammering on the anvil.

St Peter's Gate

Pigeons congregate under the plane trees at the junction of St Peter's Gate, Hounds Gate and Wheeler Gate.
Many of Nottingham's streets have the name 'Gate', which comes from the old Norse word for street.

Street entertainer
Alternating between periods of statue-like calm
and exaggerated movement, this entertainer was successful
in gaining attention and funding from many passers-by.

Balloon seller
Children cannot resist the colourful mass of balloons but they must hold tight to their purchases or they will sail up into the sky.

Albert Street
Shoppers and visitors are serenaded by a lone guitarist as they pass the Leaf Stem statue outside St Peter's church.

Victoria Street
Shoppers cross the street and the lines which mark the route of the new tramway.

Low Pavement
In the Georgian period, this was the fashionable location for a town house and there are many
attractive properties along Low and Middle Pavements.

Broad Marsh Shopping Centre
This was the second large shopping mall to be created in Nottingham, where visitors
can benefit from being out of the weather and away from the traffic.

Opposite: **Broad Marsh Shopping Centre (interior)**
Sun shines through the glass-roofed entrance which leads off from Middle Pavement.

Listergate
An avenue of trees provides welcome shade as shoppers stroll along busy Listergate.

Weekday Cross
The cross marks the site of the market for the old Saxon (English) town, when the Normans (French) had their settlement around the castle.

Jugglers, Goose Gate

This unusual and colourful shop selling games and juggling equipment for the entertainer is on Goose Gate, the street where Jesse Boot had his first herbalist shop back in the 1870s.

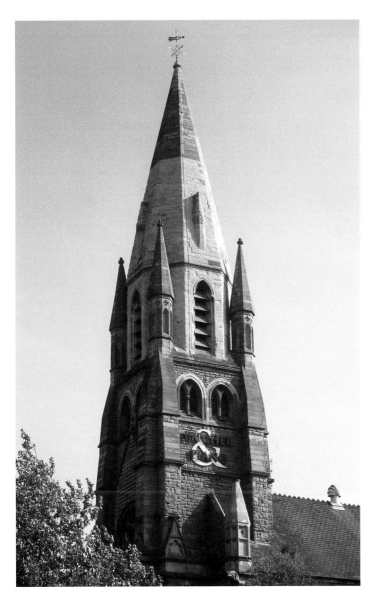

The Piano and Pitcher, High Pavement
A redundant church has found a new use as a restaurant and bar.

Floral display
A lamp post is decorated with a striking pink floral display.

Old Shire Hall, High Pavement
The old court rooms within Shire Hall and the adjoining County Gaol have been opened to the public as the Galleries of Justice,
giving visitors a chilling glimpse of crime and punishment in the nineteenth century.

Above: **Arched entrance to the County Gaol, High Pavement**
The poor stone mason who carved the lettering above this arch has attempted
to correct 'Goal' to 'Gaol'. Convicted prisoners were hanged from a scaffold
erected on the steps outside the Gaol until 1864, when public executions
were no longer considered appropriate.

Right: **Entrance to the old Police Station, High Pavement**
The wrought iron arch would have supported a gas lamp over the
entrance to the police station that adjoined Shire Hall, and it has
the initials 'VR' for *Victoria Regina*.

St Mary's church
Dating from the fifteenth century,
St Mary's is the parish church of
Nottingham and stands on a hill
at the centre of the old town.

Gravestone, St Mary's churchyard
This unusual headstone is not made of carved stone but fired clay.
This is because it was made around 1707 by a clay pipe maker
called William Sefton, and it commemorates two of his daughters.

Plaque to George Africanus, St Mary's churchyard
George John Scipio Africanus was brought from his home
in Sierra Leone to work as a servant for a wealthy business
man in Wolverhampton. However he won his freedom from
slavery and moved to Nottingham in 1784, where he
founded an employment agency for servants
and became the city's first black entrepreneur.

View of the Lace Market

This area was developed by the Victorian lace manufacturers who built their factories and warehouses along Stoney Street.
The tower of St Mary's church is visible among the buildings, old and new, which now make up this conservation area.

Opposite: **Teespoint House, Stoney Street**

Once a lace warehouse, this building has found a new use as office accommodation. Although called the Lace Market this
was not a retail market, it was simply an area with a common purpose – the manufacture and storage of lace products.

Birkin Building, Broadway
Richard Birkin, one of Nottingham's eminent lace manufacturers, owned a mansion adjoining St Mary's church, which he demolished to build his factory and warehouse complex. Many of the old buildings have found new uses as apartments, offices, bars and clubs.

Opposite: **The arched entrance to Birkin's warehouse, Broadway**
The carved lettering above the main entrance to Birkin's warehouse shows the family emblem of a bee, and the initials of the architect Thomas Chambers Hine (left), and the builders, Garland and Holland (right).

The Adams and Page lace warehouse, Stoney Street
Thomas C. Hine was the architect who designed the lace warehouse of Thomas Adams. It was built on a grand scale to impress visitors, but also included such enlightened features as heating and rest rooms for the workers, and a chapel for daily worship.

Above: **The arched entrance of the Adams Building
on St Mary's Gate**

Right: **Plaque to Thomas Adams**
Thomas Adams was one of the great lace manufacturers
of Victorian Nottingham.

The Adams Building, St Mary's Gate
The Adams Building now forms part of New College Nottingham, which offers courses in further and higher education and life-long learning. The stone carving over the window reflects the delicate patterns of the lace which would have been made there.

Lace

Lace was the staple trade of Nottingham in the second half of the nineteenth century, with finished goods being sent across the world. Trade declined after the First World War because of competition from other countries and changes in fashion and methods of production.

Plaque to John Leavers, Canning Circus

John Leavers invented a machine for making point net and warp lace. It was the development of such machines that led to the factory production of lace and net in the nineteenth century.

London Road roundabout

Displays of summer bedding plants add a splash of colour in the centre of this busy road junction. 'Nottingham in Bloom' works with many partners to provide a pleasant environment for both residents and visitors.

Opposite: **BBC Nottingham, London Road**

This modern centre for the BBC was opened in 1998, and it is the home of Radio Nottingham and East Midlands television.

The former Plumptre Hospital, Poplar Street

The almshouses with their adjoining master's house date from 1823. They were the gift of the Plumptre family for the benefit of poor widows. The building is currently used by the Royal National Institute for the Blind as their education and employment centre for the East Midlands.

Plaque on the former Plumptre Hospital

The plaque describes how the original endowment dates from 1392, with repairs carried out in 1650, 1751 and 1753, before the present building was established in the nineteenth century.

**Capital One building,
Station Street**

This building, now occupied by
Capital One, was part of the Boots
pharmaceutical complex. It was
opened in 1952 to replace an earlier
group of buildings which was
destroyed in an air raid on
the night of 8 May, 1941.

**Plaque on the
Capital One building**

The plaque commemorates
four employees of Boots Pure Drug
Co Ltd who lost their lives when the
building was bombed during
the Second World War.

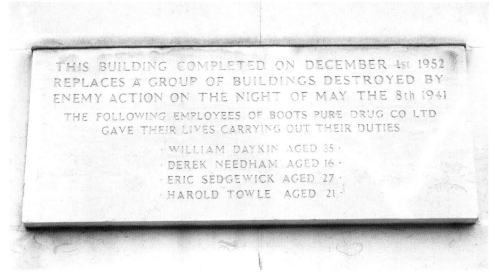

THIS BUILDING COMPLETED ON DECEMBER 1st 1952
REPLACES A GROUP OF BUILDINGS DESTROYED BY
ENEMY ACTION ON THE NIGHT OF MAY THE 8th 1941
THE FOLLOWING EMPLOYEES OF BOOTS PURE DRUG CO LTD
GAVE THEIR LIVES CARRYING OUT THEIR DUTIES

· WILLIAM DAYKIN AGED 35 ·
· DEREK NEEDHAM AGED 16 ·
· ERIC SEDGEWICK AGED 27 ·
· HAROLD TOWLE AGED 21 ·

The National Ice Centre and Arena, Bolero Square
A new and enlarged ice centre was inspired by the success of local World and Olympic Champions, Jayne Torvill and Christopher Dean. Opened in 2000, the centre has a public ice stadium and a large arena which can be covered and used as a concert hall.

Pavement, Bolero Square
The ice theme continues with the geometric patterns of snow crystals in the paved area of Bolero Square.

Sculpture, Bolero Square
The tall, stainless steel sculpture slowly rotates, its abstract design reflecting the theme of ice and skate blades with the turning movements of the skaters.

The former offices of Watson Fothergill, George Street
Fothergill Watson, who later reversed his name, became one of Nottingham's eminent nineteenth-century architects.
His offices, like many of his buildings, carry his signature, and show the use of elaborate decoration and carving.

The former National Westminster Bank, Thurland Street
Watson Fothergill was the architect of this prestigious building, which was originally the headquarters of the Nottingham and Notts Bank.

Sculptural relief panel, former National Westminster Bank
The sculptural relief panels depict aspects of Nottingham's history – its agriculture, textile working (seen here) and mining.

Thurland Hall public house, Thurland Street
Named after the now demolished Thurland Hall, this public house is over 100 years old
and still retains some of its original panes of etched glass.

Thurland Hall public house

Plaque and reflection, Pelham Street
The plaque shows that J. M. Barrie, the author of *Peter Pan*,
worked on the premises in 1883–84, when it was the office of the
Nottingham Journal. The roof turrets of the Thurland Hall public
house opposite are reflected in the window above.

Elite Building, King Street
Built in 1921 as shops and a cinema, this
building is faced in white glazed terracotta
and features statues of famous characters
from folklore and history, such as
William Shakespeare and St George.

10 Pelham Street
Built in 1903–04 for Boots the Chemists,
this is another richly-decorated building,
faced in glazed terracotta. It is now
shops and a restaurant.

The former London Road Railway Station, London Road
Designed by Thomas C. Hine this railway station was built for the Great Northern Railway Company in 1857.
Although redundant as a station, it has been restored and among its new occupants is a health and fitness club.

Guildhall, Burton Street
Once the home of the courts, the Guildhall is now used as council offices. However, below ground there is an extensive system of brick-lined passages and caves which, during the Second World War, were used as air raid shelters and an emergency headquarters for the council.

Opposite: **Victoria Centre Clock Tower, Milton Street**
When Victoria Railway Station was demolished in the 1960s, the clock tower was retained as an ornamental feature for the new Victoria Centre shopping mall.

Arboretum, Waverley Street
Spring sunshine highlights the beds of golden daffodils in the Arboretum. Opened in 1852, it was Nottingham's first public park.

Chinese Bell Tower, Arboretum

A rainbow arches over the memorial in the Arboretum. The bell was captured from the Chinese city of Canton and the canons were taken at Sebastopol during the Crimean War. They were presented to Nottingham in remembrance of the men from the town and county who served in the British Forces.

Above: **The Boots Library, Nottingham Trent University, Goldsmith Street**
The overhead wires of the tram network stand out alongside the Boots Library, one of the
newest buildings on the Nottingham Trent University city campus.

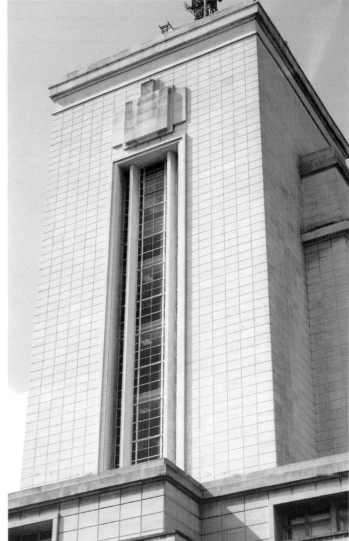

Newton Building, Nottingham Trent University, Burton Street
The towering eight storeys of the Newton Building are reflected in the glass of the Royal Concert Hall, on the opposite side
of the road. Dating from the 1950s, the building is faced in crisp white Portland stone, and it forms part
of the campus of Nottingham Trent University.

Theatre Royal, Theatre Square

Dating from 1865, the theatre was a venture by two brothers, William and John Lambert, who were textile manufacturers in the city. It is built in the classical style.

The sculpture is a modern abstract creation of the figure of Carmen worked in steel and copper.

Opposite: **Trams in Theatre Square**

Theatre Square is one of the dropping-off points for the tram system that enters the city from the north and is ideal for those visiting the surrounding entertainment venues.

Royal Concert Hall, Theatre Square
Opened in 1982, this ultra-modern complex makes extensive use of glass, which reflects the buildings which surround it.
It is a popular venue for touring orchestras, bands, dance troupes, comedians and solo artists.

The Corner House, Forman Street
This modern leisure complex attracts
visitors to its bars, restaurants
and multi-screen cinema.

Nottingham Playhouse, Wellington Circus

This modern structure of reinforced concrete was designed by Peter Moro and it contrasts, both in design and in its productions, with the Theatre Royal. The chequer-board pattern of black and white is reversed at night, and the light serves to entice visitors into the interior.

Above: **Sky Mirror, Nottingham Playhouse**
The Sky Mirror is a stainless steel concave dish
sculpture by Anish Kapoor. It measures 5.75 metres
across and reflects the tower of nearby Albert Hall.

Right: **Albert Hall, North Circus Street**
This building, named after Prince Albert, the
husband of Queen Victoria, started life as a
Methodist church. It was rebuilt in 1909 in
the style of an Edwardian theatre or music hall
and was used as a public hall for concerts and
events. It is now run by the City Council
for concerts and exhibitions.

Wellington Circus
The London plane trees of Wellington Circus are turning colour, their leaves falling and collecting
on the grassed enclosure, encircled by iron railings.

Regent Street
Thomas Chambers Hine was another of Nottingham's great Victorian architects. He was responsible
for this grand terrace in Regent Street.

Park Gates
These two gated entrances to the Park Estate serve to show that it remains privately owned.

Opposite: **Park Gates and Royal Standard House**
Built in the 1920s as a memorial to those who fell in the First World War, this nurses' home served the nearby General Hospital.
The latter has now closed and the former nurses' home has been converted into luxury apartments. The new name reflects
the fact that Charles I raised his standard near this site in 1642 at the start of the Civil War.

Park Terrace
The large houses along Park Terrace have superb views across the bowl-shaped area of ground that was once a royal forest but which was developed in the mid-nineteenth century by the Duke of Newcastle into an exclusive residential suburb.

View across the Park Estate from Park Terrace
The large architect-designed villas with their gardens and stables were favoured by the wealthy citizens of Nottingham.
Now many have been converted into flats.

Above: **Park Steps from below**

Right: **Park Steps from above**
This flight of steps, dating from 1829, leads from Park Valley
up to the Ropewalk, part of the Park Estate.

Park Tunnel
Thomas C. Hine, the architect for many of the Park's great houses, created this tunnel as a private carriage drive for the residents of the estate, giving them access onto Derby Road.

Nottingham Castle
Not a true castle, the present building was a palace built by William Cavendish, Duke of Newcastle in the seventeenth
century, after the old castle had been demolished. In 1875 the building was acquired by the City Corporation
which turned it into a museum and art gallery.

Opposite: **The Castle Gatehouse, Castle Road**
The heavily-restored thirteenth century gatehouse marks the entrance to Nottingham Castle. Unfortunately little remains
of the great medieval castle which was one of the most important in England.

View looking south-east from the Castle
The old British Waterways warehouse on the canal is visible on the right, with the offices of the *Nottingham Evening Post* in front and the station behind.

Bandstand, Nottingham Castle
The glazed wooden bandstand is a reminder of former times, when music would have been played on
Sunday afternoons as the citizens of Nottingham strolled leisurely around the grounds.

Above: **Gardens, Nottingham Castle**
The gardens around the Castle have been landscaped and they provide a pleasant green oasis in the heart of the city.

Opposite: **Statue to Albert Ball VC, Nottingham Castle**
The statue commemorates Captain Albert Ball, a young fighter pilot killed in action during the First World War, whose bravery was recognised by the award of the Victoria Cross.

**View of the Castle Museum
and Art Gallery**
The Castle was built on a cliff-top
site, taking advantage of this natural defen-
sive position. Nestling at the base of the
cliff is the Old Trip to Jerusalem public
house and in the foreground is a modern
building which forms part of the People's
College, a specialist further and higher
education college.

**West Front, Castle Museum
and Art Gallery**
The Castle holds collections of
paintings, ceramics, silver and glass in its
museum and art gallery. Visitors can
stroll out through the Tuscan colonnade
into the courtyard with its swirling leaf
pattern of pebble mosaics and enjoy
the distant views.

**Detail of courtyard mosaic,
Castle Museum and Art Gallery**

View looking south-west from the Castle
The view over Castle Boulevard picks up light industry along the Trent valley in the direction of Beeston, with the power station at Ratcliffe on Soar on the far left horizon.

Statue of Robin Hood, Castle Road
Fact or fiction, there can be few who are not familiar with the story of Robin Hood and his band of Merry Men.
The bronze statue of Robin Hood and the complementary plaques were presented to the City of Nottingham
by Philip E. F. Clay to commemorate the visit of Princess Elizabeth and the Duke of Edinburgh in 1949.

The Lace Centre, Castle Road

Known as Severns House, this wonderful old timber-framed house from the fifteenth century, was originally on Middle Pavement.
It faced demolition when the Broad Marsh Shopping Centre was being built, but was saved by Nottingham Civic Society,
who had it dismantled, restored and re-erected on its present site.

Badge of the City of Nottingham, Castle Gatehouse
The heraldic device of the city has a shield with a cross and three ducal coronets, supported on either side by royal stags, with a castle as the crest. The motto *Vivit post funera virtus* translates as 'Virtue survives death'.

Opposite: **The Castle walls and Gatehouse**
James Woodford's statue of Robin Hood stands in front of the buttressed Castle walls. The arches support the approach to the Gatehouse, the entrance to the Castle.

View of Brewhouse Yard from the Castle walls
Brewhouse Yard once had a notorious reputation as a place for those seeking refuge from the law as it lay outside
the control of the Borough. Its name comes from the Castle brewhouse which once stood there.

The Old Trip to Jerusalem public house, Castle Road

Claimed to date from 1189 and to be the oldest inn in England, the name of this famous pub is said to reflect the fact
that it was the meeting place for the Crusaders before they set off for the long journey to the Holy Land.
The back rooms are caves cut into Castle Rock.

Brewhouse Yard Museum
A row of five attractive seventeenth-century cottages has been converted into a museum depicting various aspects of life in Nottingham over the past 300 years. Visitors can enter the cellars cut into the rock behind the cottages, some of which were used as air-raid shelters during the Second World War.

Mortimer's Hole, Brewhouse Yard
This is the name for an ancient passageway linking the top of Castle Rock to Brewhouse Yard. It was reputedly used in 1330 by armed conspirators to enter the Castle and capture Roger Mortimer, the lover of Queen Isabella, widow of the murdered Edward II and mother of Edward III.

Pillar Cave, City of Caves
This complex of man-made caves is under the Broad Marsh Shopping Centre. The caves have had many uses throughout history. Pillar Cave was used as a tannery in medieval times where leather was prepared from animal skins – a long and very smelly process.

Mortimer House, Castle Road
Once the Old Castle Inn and now known as
The Castle, this public house and restaurant is a
welcome refreshment stop for visitors to the real
castle on the opposite side of the road.

Opposite: **Old boundary marker, Castle Road**
The Overseers, named on this boundary marker,
were responsible for the poor within their part
of the city. This was in the Victorian era, when
those who could not support themselves and
their families were faced with the threat
of entering the workhouse.

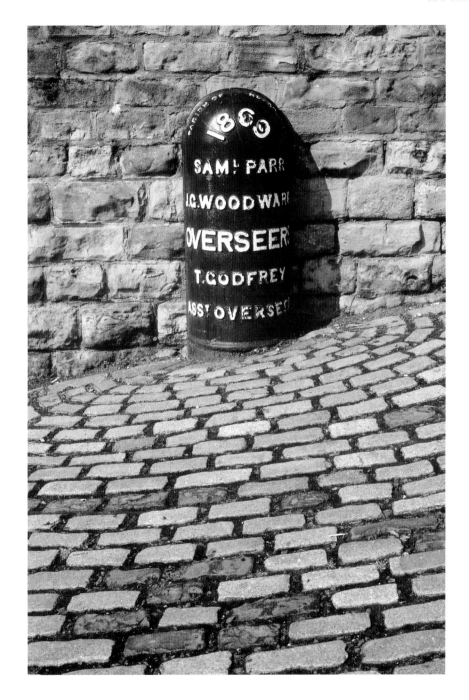

Castle Works, Brewhouse Yard
This building once held a steam engine as it was a pumping station for the city's first piped water supply, before becoming the offices of the Corporation's Water Department.

Castle Works (detail of gates)
The ornate wrought-iron gates have the initials 'NCWW' for Nottingham Corporation Water Works.

The Hicking Building, Queens Road
Once a warehouse for the firm of
Hicking, Pentecost and Co. Ltd, this
building has now been converted
into luxury apartments.

5, 7 and 9 Bridlesmith Gate
Built in 1895 as a shop and store for a
furnishing company, this tall five-storey
building is topped by ornate gables with
round windows. Many buildings in
Nottingham which date from the late
nineteenth century have these
distinctive Dutch style gables.

The Tales of Robin Hood, Maid Marian Way
This tourist attraction allows you to step back in time and experience the sights and smells
of medieval England during the time of Robin Hood.

Opposite: **Maid Marian Way**
This new road was created in the 1960s as an inner ring road to take through-traffic around the city centre.

Left **76 St James's Street**
The poet Lord Byron lived in this house on St James's Street from 1798 to 1799 when he was a boy.

Below **Plaque to Lord Byron**

19 Castle Gate
Built in 1775 as a town house, this building has been converted into offices. There are some fine Georgian houses on Castle Gate displaying the typical classical features of the eighteenth century.

The Salutation Inn, Hounds Gate
The rear part of this old public house date back to the sixteenth century. It has underground cellars cut out of the sandstone rock.

Above: **The Royal Children public house, Castle Gate**
This public house has an unusual name which is said to refer to the children
of Anne, the daughter of James II. When the Royal Family were in
danger in 1688, Anne was sent to Nottingham and her children
reputedly played with those of the pub landlord.

Right: **The sign of the Royal Children public house**

View of Castle Gate
The old lamp-post, cobbled pavement and tubs of flowers help to set off this brick town house, dating from the late eighteenth century.

Newdigate House, Castle Gate
Built around 1675 for Thomas Newdigate
this stylish house is set back behind attractive railings.
From 1705–11 it was the home of Marshal Tallard, a
French general defeated by the Duke of Marlborough
at the Battle of Blenheim. He is credited with
introducing celery to British cuisine.

Plaque on Newdigate House

The old British Waterways warehouse, Nottingham Beeston Canal
The Nottingham Canal was opened in 1796 and linked the River Trent to the wharves in the city centre and then on to Langley Mill. For a time it was extremely important for the transport of bulky and fragile goods, which would have been stored in warehouses like this, but later it suffered from competition from the railways. Many of the disused canal warehouses have been converted for other uses.

Canal boat on the Nottingham Beeston Canal
The British Waterways Board has helped restore the canal so that it can be used by pleasure boats and barges
as a navigable route through Nottingham.

Modern apartments overlooking the Nottingham Beeston Canal
The canal waterfront has become a much sought-after location, and the tow path provides a pleasant route for walkers and cyclists.

Castle Lock, Wilford Street
Locks are a necessary feature of canals to allow for an adjustment in water levels as they negotiate rising ground.

Waterfront, Canal Street

The warehouse of Fellows, Morton and Clayton, a company which once transported coal along the canal, has been converted into the Canal Museum, while their former offices have become a restaurant and bar.

Waterfront, Canal Street
Visitors enjoy their refreshments alongside moored barges on the canal.

Magistrates' Court, Carrington Street
The stylish new Magistrates' Court building is part of the development which has taken place alongside the canal.

**Inland Revenue offices,
Castle Meadow Road**
Round glass towers are a characteristic
feature of the new offices of the
Inland Revenue, which are built on an
extensive site to the south of the canal.

View of the Railway Station from London Road

In the nineteenth century, many different railway companies opened lines to serve Nottingham, but rationalisation in the twentieth century has meant that this station, built for the Midland Railway in 1904, has become the city's main railway station.

Platform 3, Railway Station
Passengers using Nottingham's busy Railway Station can easily travel to and from destinations such as
Derby, Leicester, Sheffield, Leeds and London St Pancras.

Railway Station, Carrington Street
Taxis, in their Sherwood-green livery, line up under the glazed roof of the station forecourt, ready to take passengers to their destination.

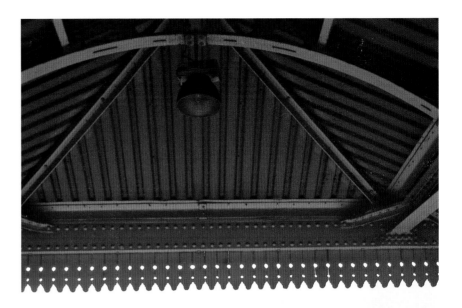

Railway roof patterns
The contrasting patterns of platform, rail, carriage and roofs stand out in strong spring sunlight.

Waterfront Plaza, Station Street
Construction is underway at the Waterfront Plaza, a mixed-use development of contemporary apartments, prestigious offices and vibrant bars, alongside Jurys Inn hotel.

Opposite: **Jurys Inn, Waterfront Plaza, Station Street**
This photograph reveals the stark modern simplicity of Nottingham's latest hotel which soars into the sky.

Notts County Football Club, Meadow Lane
Known affectionately as the 'Magpies' because of their black and
white striped kit, Notts County are acknowledged as the oldest
League Club in the world, formed in 1862.

Nottingham Forest Football Club, The City Ground
Built in 1980 as the Executive Stand, the Brian Clough Stand was renamed in 1999
in honour of the club's manager from 1975 to 1993.

Above: **Rowers on the River Trent**
Once a busy thoroughfare, the river is now used by
pleasure craft, like this crew of lady rowers training
on a Saturday afternoon.

Left: **Detail from Trent Bridge**
Pigeons roost on the decorative iron-work
which spans the river.

Above: **Trent Bridge, London Road**
Opened in 1871 and then doubled in width in 1925,
the present bridge allows pedestrians and road traffic to
cross the River Trent. The Rushcliffe Civic Centre
and Nottingham Forest Football Ground are
seen beyond the bridge.

Right: **Flood level marks under Trent Bridge**
The water levels reached in some of the worst
floods on the River Trent are recorded in
the stonework of the bridge.

Feeding swans, Victoria Embankment
Ducks, swans and geese appear from nowhere when scraps of bread are thrown into the river.

County Hall, West Bridgford
Sunlight catches the attractive green copper roof of the offices of the county council,
situated on the far bank of the River Trent in West Bridgford.

Memorial Arch and Gardens, Victoria Embankment
Sir Jesse Boot donated the land for the construction of the triumphal arch and the gardens behind. The arch is a memorial
to the citizens of Nottingham who lost their lives in the First and Second World Wars.

Suspension Bridge, River Trent
This footbridge over the River Trent hides a large pipe which carries water across to West Bridgford.

Trent Bridge Cricket Centre, Trent Bridge
Still known as the Radcliffe Road Stand, this new Trent Bridge Cricket Centre was opened by Sir Garfield Sobers in 1998.
Trent Bridge is the home of Nottinghamshire County Cricket Club and, as one of the premier grounds in the country,
it is also a venue for international Test matches.

Fox Road Stand, Trent Bridge cricket ground
The Fox Road Stand, with its cantilever roof, was unveiled in 2002 alongside the famous scoreboard. Here the Nottinghamshire county team are playing Warwickshire in the County Championship.

National Water Sports Centre, Holme Pierrepont
The 2000m long regatta lake stretches into the distance. It is used for training purposes
and for the holding of national and international sporting events.

White water rafting
An instructor helps a group of young people to experience the thrills of white water rafting.

White water slalom course, National Water Sports Centre
Water from the nearby River Trent is directed into the man-made rapids of the white water slalom course.

Kayaking
A competitor seeks to impress the judges with her skill in manoeuvring through the swirling waters of the white water course.

Wollaton Hall
Built in 1580–88 by Robert Smythson for Sir Francis Willoughby, the hall and its park are one of
Nottingham's unique features. The hall contains a natural history museum, while herds
of red and fallow deer roam the park, which is a wonderful green space for visitors to enjoy.

The Stable Block, Wollaton Hall
Dating from 1743, the Stable Block is now used as an industrial museum, gallery, shop and offices. The clock above the arched entrance has its original face and it is topped by the carved coat-of-arms of the Willoughby family.

Corner Tower, Wollaton Hall
The hall is built to a square plan, with a central hall, and projecting three-storey towers to each corner. There is much elaborate stone carving, the towers topped with obelisks and statues.

Highfields Park and the University of Nottingham, University Boulevard

Highfields Park was created in the 1920s for public recreation and enjoyment. Behind the entrance is Trent Building with its distinctive bell tower, part of the University of Nottingham. Both were founded on land donated by Sir Jesse Boot.

Bust of Sir Jesse Boot, University Boulevard
The life-size bronze bust of Sir Jesse Boot, Lord Trent, was placed at the entrance to Highfields Park in 1934,
in remembrance of one of Nottingham's leading industrialists and public benefactors.

University Park, University of Nottingham

The university is set in a landscaped park, offering pleasant walks for visitors, and plenty of space for student sport facilities.

Opposite: **Millennium Garden, University of Nottingham**

The beautifully designed Millennium Garden is a real hidden gem, a place of quiet in the midst of a busy university campus.

Raleigh Square, off Raleigh Street
The design on this door is a reminder of the Raleigh Cycle Company which took its name from the street where cycle manufacturing began in the late nineteenth century. The company, under Frank Bowden, became one of the largest employers, although it has now gone from the city.

Green's Mill, Sneinton
Recently restored as a tribute to its one-time owner, the mathematician and physicist George Green, the windmill is once again grinding flour. It is a popular visitor attraction together with its adjoining science museum.

The Forest Park and Ride
Nottingham has seven park and ride sites served by a network of buses and trams to bring sightseers, shoppers and workers into the city centre.

Passengers alighting at Station Street

Passengers arrive at Station Street on one of Nottingham's state-of-the-art trams. Many of the trams are named after famous people who have been associated with the city, like 'Robin Hood', 'D. H. Lawrence' and 'Torvill and Dean'.

Above and opposite: **The Goose Fair, the Forest Recreation Ground**
Held each year in early October, the Goose Fair is a spectacle of coloured lights, deafening noise, mouth-watering smells and whirling rides. The name is thought to originate from flocks of geese which were driven to the city for sale, but trading has given way to the pleasure fair that draws in the crowds.

View from Broad Marsh multi-storey car park
Late afternoon sunlight highlights the Lace Market area of the city as a tram descends towards its final destination at Station Street.